THE ULTIMATE
VEGAN COOKBOOK

Quick and Healthy Vegan Recipes For Every
Day incl. 30 Days Vegan Diet Challenge

1st Edition

Julia Gardner

ISBN- 9781074746964

TABLE OF CONTENTS

What is Veganism? 3

  Types of vegans 3

    Dietary vegans 3

    Ethical vegans 3

    Environmental vegans 3

  Vegan Diets 4

    Balanced vegan diets 4

  Benefits of veganism 5

    A diet rich in essential nutrients 5

    A diet that helps battle weight loss 5

    A diet that keeps type 2 diabetes away 5

    A diet that protects certain types of cancer 6

    A diet that lowers the risk of heart disease 6

    A diet that reduces pain from arthritis 6

  Equipping your kitchen 6

  Label reading 8

Recipes 11

  Recipes for Breakfast 13

    Banana bread American pancakes 14

    Classic Avocado Toast 15

    Overnight blueberry Breakfast oats 16

    Vegan Breakfast tofu wraps 17

    Low-carb avocado and tofu Breakfast salad 19

    Spinach whole-wheat tortilla wraps 20

    Overnight raspberry pudding 21

    Vegan chickpea omelette 22

    Vegan raspberry ice cream 23

    Breakfast quinoa bowl 24

  Recipes for Lunch 25

    Creamy tomatoes soup 26

    Oriental lentils salad 27

    Roasted veggies bowl 28

Protein-packed mixed beans salad 29

Fried tofu with garlicky greens beans 30

Greens and potatoes skillet 31

Vegan swede and pumpkin soup 32

Quinoa tabbouleh 33

Balkan aubergine salad 35

Refreshing brown rice salad 36

Recipes for Dinner 37

Comfort vegan stew.. 38

One-pot kidney beans and sweet potatoes stew 40

Chickpea curry with rice noodles.. 41

Curried mushrooms with quinoa 42

Stuffed mushrooms with sweet potatoes chips 44

Jamaican rice and beans... 46

Tahini mushroom penne 47

Protein-packed tofu stew 48

One-pot curry noodle soup 50

Creamy butternut squash risotto 52

30-Day Vegan Challenge **55**

DAY 1 56

DAY 2 57

DAY 3 59

DAY 4 61

DAY 5 63

DAY 6 64

DAY 7 66

DAY 8 67

DAY 9 68

DAY 10 69

DAY 11 70

DAY 12 72

DAY 13 73

DAY 14 74

DAY 15 76

DAY 16 77

DAY 17 79

DAY 18 80

DAY 19 82

DAY 20 84

DAY 21 86

DAY 22 88

DAY 23 90

DAY 24 92

DAY 25 94

DAY 26 95

DAY 27 96

DAY 28 98

DAY 29 99

DAY 30 101

Disclaimer **103**

Imprint **104**

What is Veganism?

What does it mean to be a vegan? In short, being vegan is excluding animal products from your diet. Furthermore, veganism is a philosophy, a lifestyle, where one refuses to see animals as commodity.

Types of vegans

However, people choose to be vegans for different reasons, which allows us to distinguish at least three types of vegans:

Dietary vegans

Also known as strict vegetarians, dietary vegans do not consume any animal products, including dairy products, eggs, or any animal-based or derived substances.

Ethical vegans

In addition to refraining from including in their diet any type of animal products, ethical vegans exclude the use of animals for all other purposes, including clothes, medicine, etc.

Environmental vegans

Environmental vegans do not consume animal products because they believe modern farming of animals is unsustainable and environmentally harmful.

Vegan Diets

According to the British Dietetic Association and the American Academy of Nutrition and Dietetics, well-planned veganism is applicable and suitable throughout all life stages. A vegan's diet is rich in magnesium, vitamin C, dietary fibre, folic acid, vitamin E, phytochemicals, and iron. On the other hand, vegan diets are low in saturated fat, dietary energy, cholesterol, vitamin D, long-chain omega-3 fatty acids, zinc, calcium, and vitamin B12.

Balanced vegan diets

As with any diet, an unbalanced or poorly planned vegan diet will bring about nutritional deficiencies. These deficiencies will cancel all the benefits of a well-planed diet and lead to health issues. In order to make sure the vegan diet you are following is safe, make sure you check the following:

Vitamin B12

Since this vitamin is primarily found in eggs, meat, and dairy products, vegans cannot take this vitamin from food. However, with supplements and B12-fortified foods (Nutritional yeast, plant-based milks) vegans can get sufficient amounts of vitamin B12. Why B12 matters? Because insufficient amounts of B12 lead to irreversible neurological damage and blood disorders.

Calcium

Calcium is another concern of a vegan diet since people associate calcium with animal products, such as milk, yogurt, or cheese. BUT calcium is abundant in plant-based foods, such as dark greens, almonds, soymilk, or orange juice.

Protein:

Protein is macronutrient associated with animal-based products. However, plants abound in protein just as well. Primary sources of protein for vegans include beans (lentils, chickpeas, kidney beans, beans, soy, peas), whole grains, seeds (quinoa, chia), and nuts.

Benefits of veganism

Many people embrace veganism due to its long-term health benefits. A well-balanced vegan diet can keep your body healthier longer while ensuring sustainable weight loss. Vegans are typically leaner and look younger than people who eat meat. Here are the six main health benefits of going vegan:

A diet rich in essential nutrients

Vegan diets are known to be high in certain nutrients designed to improve overall health. These nutrients include antioxidants, fibre, vitamins A, C, and E, as well as potassium, folic acid, and magnesium.

A diet that helps battle weight loss

Studies show that, compared to non-vegans, vegans have lower BMIs (body mass indexes) and are thinner. It is all due to veganism being low-calorie oriented since plants are inherently low-calorie foods compared to animal-derived foods. Therefore, veganism promotes weight loss but does not necessarily involve paying extra attention to cutting calories.

A diet that keeps type 2 diabetes away

Type 2 diabetes has become a huge health concern across the world. Eventually, type 2 diabetes impairs kidney function and triggers the onset of high blood pressure. Studies show diabetics who follow a vegan lifestyle are more successful in fighting off type 2 diabetes than diabetics who follow an ADA-recommended diet. Statistically, vegans have:

- A 50 to 78% lower risk of developing type 2 diabetes
- Higher insulin sensitivity
- Lower blood sugar and blood pressure levels

In addition, by substituting animal-based protein with plant-based protein, vegan diets significantly improve kidney function. One of the most difficult to handle side effects that diabetics must face is the symptoms of systemic distal polyneuropathy - sharp, burning pain. Several studies have demonstrated veganism to provide complete relief of these symptoms.

A diet that protects certain types of cancer

The World Health Organization states that 33.3% of cancers could be prevented by altering factors within our control, including dietary habits.

- Eating legumes lowers the risk of colorectal cancer by 9 to 18%.
- Eating 7 servings of fresh fruits and vegetables daily lowers the risk of dying from cancer by 15%.
- Eating soy-based products reduces the risk of breast cancer

In conclusion, the simple avoidance of animal products, such as processed meats, reduces significantly the risk of developing breast, colon, and prostate cancers.

A diet that lowers the risk of heart disease

Vegans eat fresh vegetables, fruits, fibre, nuts, legumes, and whole grains. A diet that is rich in these foods helps to reduce the risk of developing high blood them by 75% and the risk of dying of a heart condition by 42%. Veganism is also effective in lowering total and LDL cholesterol levels and blood sugar levels, which leads to a 46% lower risk of developing heart disease.

A diet that reduces pain from arthritis

Studies report that people who changed from an omnivorous diet to a vegan diet and suffer from any type of arthritis, including osteoarthritis and rheumatoid arthritis, show significant improvement of arthritis-related symptoms, such as joint swelling, pain, or stiffness.

Equipping your kitchen

Going vegan means mindful eating so you will most likely give up on most processed foods. You will probably cook for yourself and require certain kitchen utensils to make the transition smoother. Here is a list:

- Food processor, small blender, blender, and/or immersion blender
- Measuring tools, i.e., measuring spoons, dry and liquid measuring cups
- Veggie peeler, potato masher, grater, spiralizer, and other similar tools.
- Bamboo steamer, mesh strainer, colander
- Mortar and pestle
- Tea kettle
- Whisk, tongs, ladle, wooden spoons, silicon brush, good knives, spatulas
- Cutting board(s)
- Wok, pots, frying pans, sheet pans, oven-proof pans, and assorted lids.
- Mason jars, mixing bowls, salad bowls

As you start cooking and develop a taste for vegan foods, you will discover the exact utensils that you will need. Some need a food processor daily, some don't. It really depends on what you want to cook. Some need a julienned tool; others prefer to use a knife. Some use a blender for guacamole, others use a mortar and pestle.

Most kitchen utensils are common, and people already have them in their kitchens. It really depends on how much you used to cook before going vegan.

Important ingredients

A vegan's pantry must be well-stocked. Here are the ingredients you should make sure you always have:

- **Vegan essentials:** miso, tofu, tempeh, nutritional yeast, tahini, nori sheets, kelp, kombu, hijiki, coconut milk, coconut cream, plant-based milks, soy sauce, protein powder, seitan, agar-agar, nut butters, vegan-friendly vitamins (especially B12)
- **Essential fruits and veggies:** frozen fruits, frozen veggies, lemons, bananas, cashews, greens, sweet potatoes, mushrooms, berries, avocados, bell peppers
- **"Meat" replacements:** veggie broth, vegan mayo, vegan cheeses, vegan yogurts, agar-agar (vegan gelatin), vegan chocolate (dark chocolate)

- **Canned beans:** lentils, chickpeas, pinto, black, kidney, and cannellini beans, edamame, peas
- **Grains:** Brown, wild, and white rice, quinoa, farro, spelt, bulgur, millet, oats
- **Flours:** almond flour, coconut flour, wholegrain flours, plain flour, etc.
- **Seeds:** chia seeds, flax seeds, cumin seeds, sesame seeds, pumpkin seeds, sunflower seeds, etc.
- Nuts: walnuts, almonds, macadamia nuts, Brazilian nuts, cashews, pistachios, pine nuts, etc.
- Pastas: soba noodles, rice noodles, egg-free pasta.
- Dried fruit: dried apricots, raisins, cranberries, dates.
- Sweeteners: maple syrup, agave syrup, applesauce, date syrup, pomegranate syrup, blackstrap molasses, tapioca.
- Spices: salt, pepper, curry, paprika, cayenne pepper, turmeric, cumin, bay leaves, onion and garlic powder, garam masala, curry paste, etc.
- Oils: extra-virgin olive oil, coconut oil, sesame oil, canola oil, and other vegetable oils.
- Vinegars: apple cider vinegar, white and red wine vinegars, rice vinegar
- Other canned goods: peeled tomatoes, tomato concentrate, chopped tomatoes, tomato sauce

Label reading

Label reading is essential for a vegan. In the beginning, it may seem like a daunting task, but soon you will get familiar with the ingredients. The key is to go for products with short ingredient lists.

- Foods that you must avoid: beef, poultry, pork, game, fowl, animal seafood, dairy, eggs, or any other animal-derived products.
- Hidden animal-based Ingredients: albumen, beeswax, allantoin, blood, bone china, bone char, carmine, castoreum, casein, cochineal, emu oil, elastin, gelatine, isinglass,

honey, keratin, lanolin, lactic acid, lard, retinol, rennet, shellac, tallow, squalene, yellow grease, whey.

- Products to pay attention to: wine, beer, sugar

- Ingredients that may be vegan: Allantoin, retinol, lactic acid, and squalene

- Controversial Ingredients: silk, honey, insect products, or palm oil

- Meat replacements: it is best to cook your own food than buy any processed foods. From an environmental perspective, processing damages the environment.

RECIPES

Recipes for Breakfast

Banana bread American pancakes

Prep Time: 15 minutes | Cook time: 15 minutes | Serves: 2
Nutrition per serving:
Calories: 477 | Carbs: 85 g | Fibres: 4 g | Fat: 11 g | Protein: 8 g

Ingredients:

- 1 banana (very ripe, large)
- 3/4 cup plant-based milk (unsweetened)
- 1 tsp. coconut oil
- 1 cup plain flour
- 1 tsp. maple syrup
- 1 ½ tsps. baking powder
- ¼ cup chocolate chips (vegan)
- 1 tbsp. hazelnut meal

Preparation:

1. Use a fork or potato masher to mash the banana into a fine puree. Incorporate the milk, oil, and maple syrup. Combine the baking powder and flour and fold in the banana mixture. Incorporate the hazelnut meal and chocolate chips. Give it a quick whisk.

2. Spray or brush a pancake pan with vegetable oil. Place on moderate heat. Use an ice cream scoop to add the batter to the hot pan. Allow to cook until bubbles form in the centre of the pancake. Flip the pancake and let it cook on the other side.

3. Repeat the previous step until you finish all the batter. As you cook each pancake, stack them on a platter. Serve them with sliced banana on top, a drizzle of maple syrup and a sprinkle of hazelnut meal!

Classic Avocado Toast

Prep Time: 2 minutes | Cook time: 2 minutes | Serves: 1
Nutrition per serving:
Calories: 377 | Carbs: 35 g | Fibres: 13 g | Fat: 26 g | Protein: 7.7 g

Ingredients:

- 1 slice seeded wholegrain bread
- 1 medium avocado (skinned and pitted)
- Salt and pepper
- Lime juice

Preparation:

1. Place the bread slice into a toaster and toast to preference.
2. In a small bowl, mash the avocado with a fork to desired consistency. Season with salt and pepper. Spread onto the bread slice.
3. Drizzle the avocado with lemon juice and garnish to taste!
4. Top with sliced tomatoes, diced tofu, sliced jalapenos, mixed seeds, or nuts!

Overnight blueberry Breakfast oats

Prep Time: 10 minutes | Cook time: 10 minutes | Serves: 1
Nutrition per serving:
Calories: 404 | Carbs: 82 g | Fibres: 10 g | Fat: 5.3 g | Protein: 9.9 g

Ingredients:

- 60 g rolled oats
- 180 ml oat milk (unsweetened)
- 75 g frozen blueberries
- 35 g fresh blueberries
- 1 tsp. agave syrup
- ½ tsp. coconut flakes
- ¼ tsp. ground vanilla beans

Preparation:

1. Pour ¾ of the oat milk in a glass jar over with the rolled oats. Mix until combined. Transfer to fridge and let the oats sit overnight.
2. The next morning, place a pot on moderate heat and add the frozen blueberries, agave syrup, and vanilla. Stir and give the blueberry mix 10 minutes for the sauce to reach desired thickness. Remove the blueberries "jam" from heat.
3. Incorporate remaining oat milk into the overnight rolled oats. Stir the oats and oat milk until well combined. Top with the blueberry sauce (warm). Decorate the pudding with the fresh berries and sprinkle coconut flakes! Enjoy!

Vegan Breakfast tofu wraps

Prep Time: 10 minutes | Cook time: 10 minutes | Serves: 2
Nutrition per serving:
Calories: 407 | Carbs: 38 g | Fibres: 7 g | Fat: 22 g | Protein: 19 g

Ingredients:

- 1 tsp. olive oil
- ½ tsp. ground paprika
- 250g tofu (firm, low sodium, crumbled)
- ½ tsp. ground cumin
- Salt and pepper
- ½ tsp. cayenne pepper
- 30g sun-dried tomatoes (finely chopped)
- 65 g green olives (small variety, pitted)
- 1 tbsp. fresh basil or parsley (finely chopped)
- 2 whole wheat tortilla wraps
- ½ avocado (without skin, pitted, and diced), divided
- ¼ yellow bell pepper (deseeded, finely sliced, divided)
- 10 baby plum tomatoes (halved), divided
- lettuce leaves (hard core removed)

Preparation:

1. In a medium pan, heat the olive oil on moderate heat. Add the crumbled tofu and seasonings. Stir well and give the tofu 5 minutes to cook.
2. Add the sun-dried tomatoes, chopped parsley or basil, and green olives to the pan. Mix and let the mixture warm up for 3 more minutes on moderate to low heat. Remove from heat.
3. Place the tortillas in the microwave and allow 5 seconds to soften and warm up. Similarly, place the tortilla wraps in a pan and heat until warm and soft.

4. Remove the stems from the lettuce leaves if any. Arrange the leaves on the tortilla wraps. Add the raw veggies (bell pepper, tomatoes, avocado). Top with the scrambled tofu. Fold in the sides and roll.

5. Place the tofu wraps in the pan and let them cook for one minute on each side. Transfer the wraps to a cutting board, slice in half, and enjoy!

Low-carb avocado and tofu Breakfast salad

Prep Time: 5 minutes | Cook time: 5 minutes | Serves: 1
Nutrition per serving:
Calories: 400 | Carbs: 15 g | Net carbs: 5.22 g | Fibres: 9.3 g | Fat: 33 g | Protein: 15 g

Ingredients:

- 100 g firm tofu (2 slices)
- 1 small avocado (pitted, cubed)
- 50 g cucumber (peel on, diced)
- 100 g cherry tomatoes (halved)
- 1 spring of green onions (finely sliced)
- Salt and pepper to taste
- 1 tbsp. extra virgin olive oil

Preparation:

1. Place a small saucepan on moderate heat. Brush the pan with olive oil. Place the tofu slices in the pan and let them brown on each side. Remove from heat and place on a cutting board to cool slightly. Once cooled, cube the tofu and set aside.
2. Meanwhile, prepare the avocado and veggies. Add them to a medium-sized bowl. Add the cubed tofu and olive oil. Toss to combine. Season with salt and pepper!

Tips!!! Place the tofu slices in kitchen towels to extract moisture. For a hot morning salad, chop jalapeno pepper (pickled) and stir into the salad!

Spinach whole-wheat tortilla wraps

Prep Time: 15 minutes | Cook time: 15 minutes | Serves: 2
Nutrition per serving:
Calories: 419 | Carbs: 44 g | Fibres: 11 g | Fat: 17 g | Protein: 18 g

Ingredients:

- 1 whole-wheat tortilla wrap
- 1tbsp. extra virgin olive oil
- 300 g baby spinach
- ½ medium red onion (finely chopped)
- 1 tbsp. tomato concentrate
- Salt and pepper to taste

Preparation:

1. Heat olive oil in a medium sized frying pan. Add the diced red onion and fry on low heat until translucent.
2. Meanwhile, add the baby spinach to a pot of lightly salted boiling water. Let boil for 1 minute. Use a slotted spoon to remove the spinach from the water. Place in a strainer to cool and drain for 2 minutes.
3. Add the drained spinach to the frying pan over the fried onion. Stir in to combine and increase heat to moderate. Allow 1 more minute to cook. Incorporate the tomato paste. Let spinach cook for one more minute or until the excess liquid has evaporated. Remove from heat.
4. Heat the tortilla wrap in the microwave until soft and warm. Place the spinach mixture on top. Fold in the sides and roll. Enjoy!

Overnight raspberry pudding

Prep Time: 10 minutes | Cook time: 10 minutes | Serves: 1

Nutrition per serving:

Calories: 342 | Carbs: 49 g | Fibres: 22 g | Fat: 15 g | Protein: 9 g

Ingredients:

- 130 g raspberries (fresh)
- 20 g raspberries (fresh) for decoration
- 250 ml almond milk (unsweetened)
- 1 tbsp. agave syrup
- 3 tbsps. chia seeds

Preparation:

1. Place the raspberries (except for the décor ones) in a blender or food processor. Pour in the plant-based milk and the agave syrup. Mix to desired consistency!
2. Transfer the raspberry and almond milk mixture to a glass jar. Stir in the chia seeds until well combined. Give it 30 minutes to rest at room temperature. Stir again. Place in the fridge for 4 hours or overnight for the pudding to thicken.
3. The next morning, remove from fridge and decorate with the fresh raspberries. Enjoy!

Vegan chickpea omelette

Prep Time: 15 minutes | Cook time: 15 minutes | Serves: 2

Nutrition per serving:

Calories: 360 | Carbs: 42 g | Fibres: 11 g | Fat 14.4 g | Protein: 18 g

Ingredients:

- Chickpea omelette
- ½ cup chickpea flour
- 2 tbsps. nutritional yeast
- ¼ tsp. baking powder
- ¼ tsp. ground turmeric
- ¼ tsp. paprika
- ¼ tsp. black pepper
- ¾ cup water
- 1 tbsp. vegetable oil, for frying

- 1 tbsp. soy sauce
- Stir-fried veggies
- 1 tsp. vegetable oil
- 1 garlic clove, minced
- ½ medium onion (julienned)
- 1 cup broccoli florets
- ½ red bell pepper (finely sliced)
- Salt and pepper to taste

Preparation:

1. Mix the ingredients for the omelette in a bowl. Give the "omelette" batter 10 minutes to rest at room temperature.
2. Brush a medium-sized pan with vegetable oil and heat on moderate heat. Use a small ladle to pour ½ of the batter into the pan. Let it cook until bubbles start forming in the centre and the edges are set. Flip the omelette and cook for 2 more minutes on the other side. Remove from pan onto a plate. Repeat this step with the remaining batter.
3. Add the vegetable oil for the stir-fried veggies to the same pan. Heat on moderate heat and add the veggie. Fry to desired tenderness. Season with salt and pepper to taste and give it a quick stir. Transfer onto the chickpea omelettes. Fold and serve!

Vegan raspberry ice cream

Prep Time: 5 minutes | Cook time: 5 minutes | Serves: 2
Nutrition per serving:
Calories: 335 | Carbs: 85 g | Fibres: 11 g | Fat: 1 g | Protein: 4 g

Ingredients:

- 3 bananas (peeled, chopped, frozen)
- 40 g frozen raspberries
- 1 tbsp. almond butter
- 1 tsp. maple or agave syrup
- 1 ½ tsps. water
- Fresh raspberries for décor

Preparation:

1. Place frozen fruit in a food processor and blend into a smooth cream.
2. Transfer the cream into a serving bowl.
3. Mix the almond butter, water, and maples syrup into a smooth sauce. Drizzle over the ice cream bowl and top with fresh raspberries.

Breakfast quinoa bowl

Prep Time: 5 minutes | Cook time: 15 minutes | Serves: 4

Nutrition per serving:

Calories: 360 | Carbs: 42 g | Fibres: 11 g | Fat: 14.4 g | Protein: 18 g

Ingredients:

- 500 ml water
- 170 g raw quinoa
- ¼ tsp. salt
- 180 ml plant-based milk of choice
- 1 large banana (ripe and mashed)
- 3 tbsps. cocoa powder
- 3 tbsps. peanut butter
- 2 tbsps. maple syrup

Preparation:

1. Bring a pot with of 2 cups of lightly salted water to a light boil. Add the quinoa to the boiling water. Place a lid to cover the pot and let boil on moderate heat for 20 minutes or until fluffy and the water has evaporated.

2. Reduce heat to low and pour the milk into the pot. Stir in the mashed banana, peanut butter, agave or maple syrup, and cocoa powder. Let simmer for 2 minutes until warmed through. Taste and add more milk or more maple syrup if needed.

3. Top with banana slices, chocolate chunks, or fresh raspberries. Serve immediately. Enjoy!

Recipes for Lunch

Creamy tomatoes soup

Prep Time: 5 minutes | Cook time: 15 minutes | Serves: 1
Nutrition per serving:
Calories: 542 | Carbs: 31 g | Fibres: 6 g | Fat: 39 g | Protein: 16 g

Ingredients:

- 1 tbsp. olive oil
- 1 red onion (julienned)
- 1 coloured bell pepper (finely sliced)
- 1 garlic clove (minced)
- 1 can chopped tomatoes
- 100 g silken tofu

- ¼ can full fat coconut milk
- Salt and pepper to taste
- 1 bay leaf
- Cayenne pepper to taste
- Freshly chopped parsley to serve

Preparation:

1. Add the onions, bell pepper, and minced garlic. Let fry on low heat until tender but not soft. Remove from heat.
2. Place all remaining ingredients in a food processor. Pulse until smooth. Add in the fried veggies and pulse to desired consistency. Transfer to a small pot.
3. Add in the bay leaf. Place the soup on moderate heat. Bring it to a gentle boil. Give it 10 minutes to warm through. Season with salt and pepper and flavour with the cayenne pepper to preference!
4. Serve hot with freshly chopped parsley!

Oriental lentils salad

Prep Time: 10 minutes | Cook time: 0 minutes | Serves: 2
Nutrition per serving:
Calories: 375 | Carbs: 48.5 g | Fibres: 12.5 g | Fat: 16 g | Protein: 11.5 g

Ingredients:

- 1 can green lentils
- 10 spring onions
- 200 g tomatoes
- 10 fresh parsley sprigs
- 2 tbsps. extra virgin olive oil
- Seeds of 1 pomegranate
- Lemon juice
- 2 garlic cloves (minced)
- Salt and pepper to taste

Preparation:

1. Rinse the green lentils and drain well. Place in a large glass bowl.
2. Chop finely the tomatoes, green onions, and parsley. Add to the lentils bowl.
3. Add the pomegranate seeds to the lentils and vegetables bowl. Toss and combine.
4. Add the olive oil, salt and pepper, and minced garlic. Give it another quick mix! Enjoy!

Roasted veggies bowl

Prep Time: 5 minutes | Cook time: 20-25 minutes | Serves: 2
Nutrition per serving:
Calories: 280 | Carbs: 29.5 g | Fibres:7.5 g | Fat: 15 g | Protein: 7 g

Ingredients:

- 200 g Brussel sprouts (trimmed and stemmed)
- 200 g sweet potatoes (peeled and cubed)
- 1 large red onion (peeled and eighths)
- 200 g cauliflower florets
- 2 tbsps. olive oil
- Salt and pepper to taste
- Lemonjuice
- 1tbsp. mixed seeds

Preparation:

1. Pre-heat oven to 170°C (340°F).
2. Arrange the veggies on a baking tray like a cob salad. Drizzle with the olive oil. Season with salt and pepper. Mix the veggies to coat with the olive oil and seasonings.
3. Transfer tray to oven and let cook until the veggies are tender. They should be done in about 20-25 minutes.
4. Remove the veggies from the oven and give them 5 minutes to cool. Transfer to serving bowls. Season with a touch of lemon juice and a pinch of salt and pepper.
5. Serve with warm pita! Enjoy!

Protein-packed mixed beans salad

Prep Time: 10 minutes | Cook time: 0 minutes | Serves: 1
Nutrition per serving:
Calories: 446 | Carbs: 59 g | Fibres: 19 g | Fat: 17 g | Protein: 17 g

Ingredients:

- ½ cup canned mixed beans in water
- ¼ can chickpeas
- 1 cup green cabbage (finely sliced)
- 1 garlic clove (minced)
- 1 small carrot(grated)
- 1 green onion stalk (finely sliced)
- ½ English cucumber (seeded, cubed)

- 200g cherry tomatoes
- Vinaigrette
- 1 tbsp.extra virgin olive oil
- 1 tsp.lemon juice
- 1 tsp. mustard (unsweetened)
- Salt and pepper to taste

Preparation:

1. Rinse and drain the mixed beans and chickpeas. Transfer to a glass bowl.
2. Add the rest of the veggies to the same bowl. Give it a quick mix.
3. Place all the ingredients for the vinaigrette/dressing in a bowl and whisk them until creamy and frothy. Pour over the beans salad and mix to combine!
4. Serving suggestions: serve with rye or multigrain crispbread.

Fried tofu with garlicky greens beans

Prep Time: 5 minutes | Cook time: 20 minutes | Serves: 2
Nutrition per serving:
Calories: 545 | Carbs: 32 g | Fibres: 13.5 g | Fat: 29.5 g | Protein: 32.5 g

Ingredients:

- 400 g firm tofu (8 slices)
- Cayenne pepper to taste
- 3 garlic cloves (minced)
- 400g green beans (fresh)

- 2 whole-wheat tortilla wraps
- 2 tbsps. extra virgin olive oil
- Salt and pepper to taste

Preparation:

1. Tofu: Heat ½ olive oil in a medium-sized pan on moderate heat. Place the tofu slices into the pan and allow 2-3 minutes to fry. While the tofu fries on one side, brush some of the oil in the pan on the upper side. Sprinkle with cayenne pepper to taste. Flip and fry on the other side. Remove from pan and onto a cutting board to cool.
2. ***Green beans:*** In a wok, add remaining olive oil and heat on moderate heat. Add the green beans and allow 8-10 minutes to cook with the lid on. Remove the lid and give it 3 more minutes to cook to desired tenderness. Stir in the minced garlic and season to taste. Give it a good stir and let it cook for 2-3 more minutes.
3. ***Tortilla wraps:*** Place the tortilla wraps in the microwave and set it to 1 minute. It should turn crispy. Reduce or increase time depending on microwave.
4. ***Serving:*** Serve the garlicky green beans with hot and crispy tortilla wraps and spicy tofu. Enjoy!

Greens and potatoes skillet

Prep Time: 5 minutes | Cook time: 20 minutes | Serves: 2
Nutrition per serving:
Calories: 545 | Carbs: 32 g | Fibres: 13.5 g | Fat: 29.5 g | Protein: 32.5 g

Ingredients:

- 1 tbsp. extra virgin olive oil
- ½ yellow onion (finely chopped)
- 300 g baby spinach and baby kale mix (chopped)
- 1 tbsp. tomato paste, double concentrate
- 1 tsp. garlic powder
- 100 g Marabel potatoes
- 100 g sweet potatoes
- 5 cashew nuts (crushed)
- Salt and pepper to taste

Preparation:

1. Peel and cube the potatoes and boil them to desired tenderness. Sweet potatoes are likely to be done quicker. Remove from water and set aside. Potatoes should be soft, but not mushy.
2. Meanwhile, add the olive oil to a medium-sized frying pan and heat on moderate heat. Add the onions and let fry on low heat until translucent. Stir in the kale and spinach mix. Increase heat to moderate and let cook until wilted. Add in the tomato concentrate and cook for 2 more minutes.
3. Transfer the potatoes from the pot to the frying pan. Mix to combine. Season with salt and pepper and garlic powder to taste. Let warm through for another minute.
4. Transfer to plates and top with the crushed cashew nuts. Enjoy!

Vegan swede and pumpkin soup

Prep Time: 10 minutes | Cook time: 30 minutes | Serves: 1
Nutrition per serving:
Calories: 322 | Carbs: 39 g | Fibres: 9.3 g | Fat: 17 g | Protein: 7.3 g

Ingredients:

- 1 garlic clove (peeled)
- 1 shallot (peeled, cut into wedges)
- 150 g swede (peeled and cubed)
- 150g pumpkin (peeled and cubed)
- 1 tbsp. olive oil
- ¼ litre vegetable broth
- Salt and pepper to taste
- Juice of ¼ lime
- 15 g pumpkin seeds (roasted)

Preparation:

1. Heat the oven to 190°C (380°F).
2. Add the swede, pumpkin, shallot and garlic to a baking dish. Drizzle with the olive oil and sprinkle with salt and pepper. Toss to combine and roast for half an hour. Remove from oven and transfer to a pot.
3. Pour the vegetable broth on top of the roasted veggies and bring to a light boil on moderate heat. Reduce heat and allow 5 minutes to simmer. Remove from stove.
4. Add the lime juice and seasonings and blend with an immersion blender into a smooth soup.
5. Transfer to bowls and top with roasted pumpkin seeds.

Quinoa tabbouleh

Prep Time: 10 minutes | Cook time: 30 minutes | Serves: 2
Nutrition per serving:
Calories: 418 | Carbs: 35 g | Fibres: 6 g | Fat: 29.5 g | Protein: 7 g

Ingredients:

- Quinoa:
- 1 cup quinoa, rinsed well
- 1 ¼ cup water
- ½ tsp. salt
- Veggies
- 2 Persian cucumbers (deseeded, cubed)
- ½ mini red bell pepper (finely sliced)
- ½ mini yellow bell pepper (finely sliced)
- ½ mini orange bell pepper (finely sliced)
- 300 cherry tomatoes (quartered)
- ½ cup fresh mint (chopped)
- 1 cup flat-leaf parsley (chopped)
- 2 green onion stalks (finely sliced)
- Vinaigrette
- 1 garlic clove (minced)
- 2 tbsps. lemon juice
- ¼ cup olive oil
- Salt and pepper to taste

Preparation:

1. Quinoa: Place the quinoa with the salt and water in a small pot over moderate-high heat. Bring to a boil and lower heat to moderate-low. Cover with a lid and let simmer until quinoa is tender or circa 10 minutes. Remove from heat and let sit with the lid on for another 5 minutes.
2. Meanwhile, whisk the lemon, olive oil, and garlic, into a smooth vinaigrette. Season with salt and pepper.

3. Drain quinoa and spread on an oven tray lined with parchment paper. Let cool completely. Once cooled, add the quinoa to a large bowl. Stir in the veggies and drizzle with the vinaigrette. Toss to combine! Divide in two bowls and enjoy!

4. **Serving:** Enjoy with crispbread of choice or warm tortilla wraps!

Balkan aubergine salad

Prep Time: 20 minutes | Cook time: 30 minutes | Serves: 2
Nutrition per serving:
Calories: 322 | Carbs: 47.5 g | Fibres: 11 g | Fat: 15 g | Protein: 5.5 g

Ingredients:

- 400 g char-grilled aubergines (jarred)
- 2 red onions (cut in ½-inch thick slices)
- 3 roasted bell peppers (drained, seeded, finely sliced)
- 150 cherry tomatoes
- 2 tbsps. pomegranate sauce
- 2 tbsps. extra virgin olive oil
- Fresh parsley (finely chopped)
- Lemon juice
- Salt to taste

Preparation:

1. Heat oven to 230°C (450°F).
2. Place the red onions and cherry tomatoes on a baking sheet-lined oven tray and let roast for 10-15 minutes. Remove the cherry tomatoes and let the red onions caramelize lightly in the oven. Should be sticky when done. Transfer to a cutting board and let cool. Cut the roast tomatoes in halves and separate the onions into rings.
3. Place the aubergines in a salad bowl. Add in the bell peppers, roast tomatoes, caramelized onions, and freshly chopped parsley. Season with salt and stir in the olive oil and pomegranate sauce. Mix to combine and adjust to taste with lemon juice. Enjoy with warm pita bread and crushed roasted pistachio nuts!

Refreshing brown rice salad

Prep Time: 10 minutes | Cook time: 20 minutes | Serves: 2

Nutrition per serving:

Calories: 450 | Carbs: 52 g | Fibres: 7.5 g | Fat: 20.5 g | Protein: 8.5 g

Ingredients:

- 100g parboiled brown rice
- 200 g heirloom tomatoes
- 1medium red onion
- 1 English cucumber
- 50g green olives (pitted)

- 50g rocket leaves
- Fresh dill (chopped)
- Fresh parsley (chopped)
- Lemon juice to taste

Salt and pepper to tastePreparation:

1. Cook the parboiled rice as per instructions. Divide the rice and transfer to two serving bowls. Top with equal amounts of rocket leaves.
2. Slice and dice the tomatoes, onion, and cucumber into small cubes. Divide the fresh veggies and place onto the rice and rocket bowls.
3. Chop dill and parsley to desired fineness. Place on top of the freshly chopped veggies. Season each bowl with salt and pepper.
4. Drizzle 1 tbsp. of olive oil on each bowl. Season with salt and pepper. Give the bowls a quick mix. Taste and add lemon juice to preference!
5. Enjoy!

Recipes for Dinner

Comfort vegan stew

Prep Time: 15 minutes | Cook time: 20 minutes | Serves: 4
Nutrition per serving:
Calories: 315 | Carbs: 55 g | Fibres: 10 g | Fat: 7.5 g | Protein: 7.5 g

Ingredients:

- 2 tbsps. Extra-virgin olive oil
- 2 yellow bell peppers (seeds removed, finely sliced)
- 1 large yellow onion (finely chopped)
- 2 medium carrots (peeled, finely sliced)
- 1 large aubergine (chopped to bite-size pieces)
- 2 large red potatoes (peeled, cubed to bite-sized pieces)
- 1tsp. ground cumin
- 1 tsp. smoked paprika
- 1 tsp. black pepper
- Vegetable broth as needed
- 1 can chopped tomatoes
- Cayenne pepper to taste
- Salt to taste
- Freshly chopped parsley

Preparation:

1. Cube the aubergine into bite-size pieces. Place on a sheet pan lined with kitchen towels. Sprinkle with salt. Let sit for 15 minutes.

1. Meanwhile, place olive oil in a medium-sized wok. Add the finely diced onions, bell pepper strips, and carrot slices. Give it 2 minutes to cook on moderate heat. Reduce heat and let cook for 5 more minutes.

2. Add the cubed potatoes and seasonings, except for cayenne pepper. Stir to combine. Add the vegetable broth or water to cover the potatoes. Place a lid on the wok, increase heat to moderate, and let cook for 15 minutes.

3. When the potatoes are almost done, add the chopped tomatoes to the wok along with the aubergine cubes. Stir and allow to cook with the lid on for 10-15 minutes or until the aubergine are tender, but not mushy. Taste and season with cayenne pepper to taste and salt if needed.

4. Serve cold or hot or cold with warm whole-wheat tortilla or crispbread, and freshly chopped parsley!

One-pot kidney beans and sweet potatoes stew

Prep Time: 10 minutes | Cook time: 30 minutes | Serves: 4

Nutrition per serving:

Calories: 288 | Carbs: 46.5 g | Fibres: 12.25 g | Fat: 7.5 g | Protein: 10 g

Ingredients:

- 2 tbsps.extra-virgin olive oil
- 1 bell pepper (diced)
- 1 yellow onion (finely chopped)
- 1 large carrot (finely cubed)
- 2 sweet potatoes (peeled and cubed)
- 1 can beans of choice in water
- 1 can chopped tomatoes (low sodium)
- Fresh parsley
- 2 bay leaves
- Salt and pepper to taste

Preparation:

1. Place olive oil in a medium-sized wok over moderate heat. Add the finely diced onions, bell pepper strips, and carrot slices. Let cook for 2 minutes. Reduce heat and let cook for 5 more minutes.
2. Add the cubed sweet potatoes and seasonings. Give it a stir. Pour the vegetable broth to cover the sweet potatoes. Increase heat and let cook with the lid on until the sweet potatoes are tender but not mushy.
3. Add the chopped tomatoes and give it a stir. Let cook for 5 more minutes. Garnish with fresh parsley and serve with bread of choice!

Chickpea curry with rice noodles

Prep Time: 5 minutes | Cook time: 20 minutes | Serves: 4
Nutrition per serving:
Calories: 357 | Carbs: 34 g | Fibres: 6.5 g | Fat: 22.5 g | Protein: 9 g

Ingredients:

- 2 tbsps. extra-virgin olive oil
- 1 yellow onion
- 1 tbp. ground cumin
- 1 tbp. ground paprika
- 1 tbp. turmeric powder
- 1 tbp. curry powder
- ½ can chopped tomatoes
- 1 can chickpeas (drained)

- Vegetable broth as needed
- 1 can coconut milk (previously refrigerated for 4 hours)
- 150g baby spinach leaves
- 200g rice noodles
- Salt and pepper
- Freshly chopped parsley

Preparation:

1. Place olive oil in a medium-sized wok over moderate heat. Add the finely diced onions and let cook for until translucent. Add the seasonings and stir until well incorporated.
2. Add the chopped tomatoes and chickpeas. Add the solid coconut milk from the can. Stir gently and let cook for 10-15 minutes until the curry has thickened to desired consistency. Stir in the chopped baby spinach towards the end and let cook for 5 more minutes. Season to taste and remove from heat.
3. Meanwhile, cook the rice noodles as per directions. Drain and place in serving bowls. Transfer curry on top of the noodles and serve with freshly chopped peppers.

Curried mushrooms with quinoa

Prep Time: 10 minutes | Cook time: 20 minutes | Serves: 4
Nutrition per serving:
Calories: 415 | Carbs: 42 g | Fibres: 8.25 g | Fat: 23.75 g | Protein: 12.75 g

Ingredients:

- 2 tbsps. extra-virgin olive oil
- 1 medium yellow onion
- 1 tbp. ground cumin
- 1 tbp. ground paprika
- 1 tbp. turmeric powder
- 1 tbp. curry powder
- ½ can chopped tomatoes
- 500g chestnut mushrooms (quartered)
- Vegetable broth as needed

- 1 can coconut milk (solid parts only)
- 150 g baby spinach (chopped)
- Salt and pepper
- Quinoa
- 1 ¼ cup water
- 1 cup dry quinoa
- ½ tsp. salt
- Serving
- Freshly chopped parsley

Preparation:

1. Place olive oil in a medium-sized wok over moderate heat. Add the finely diced onions and let cook for until translucent. Add the seasonings and stir to combine.
2. Stir in the chopped tomatoes and quartered mushrooms. Drain the coconut milk and stir in the solid part. Let cook for 10-15 minutes until the curry has thickened to desired consistency. When almost done, stir in the chopped baby spinach and let cook for 5 more minutes. Season to taste and remove from heat.

3. Meanwhile, place the quinoa with the water and salt in a small pot over moderate-high heat. Bring to a boil. Lower heat to moderate-low and cover with a lid. let simmer circa 10 minutes or until quinoa is tender. Remove from heat and let sit with the lid on for another 5 minutes. Fluff with a fork.

4. Place the quinoa in bowls. Add the curried mushrooms on top. Serve with freshly chopped parsley!

Stuffed mushrooms with sweet potatoes chips

Prep Time: 10 minutes | Cook time: 30 minutes | Serves: 2

Nutrition per serving:

Calories: 330 | Carbs: 44.5 g | Fibres: 10 g | Fat: 15 g | Protein: 10 g

Ingredients:

- 8 large portabella mushroom caps
- 2 tbsps. extra virgin olive oil
- The stems of the portabella mushroom stems (chopped finely)
- 1 carrot (grated)
- 1small red onion (chopped finely)
- 2 springs green onions (sliced finely)
- 1 large sweet potato (peeled and sliced into chips)
- 1 mini bell pepper (diced)
- Salt and pepper
- Olive oil spray

Preparation:

1. Heat oven to 230°C (450°F).
2. Place olive oil in a small pan over moderate heat. Add in the onions, diced mushrooms stems, grated carrot, and diced bell pepper. Season with salt and pepper. Stir gently and let cook for up to 5 minutes. Add in the chopped parsley and give it a quick stir. Remove from heat.
3. Stuff the mushroom caps with the mushroom mixture. Place the mushrooms on an oven-safe dish. Place in the oven on the middle rack. Give the mushrooms 20 minutes to cool until tender. Transfer stuffed mushrooms to plates.

4. Place the sweet potatoes in a bowl and season with salt and pepper. Spray or drizzle a little olive oil and toss to coat. Arrange the sliced sweet potatoes on the same oven tray. Place the tray in the oven. Cook to desired crispiness. Remove from oven and move onto plates! Enjoy!

Jamaican rice and beans

Prep Time: 5 minutes | Cook time: 25 minutes | Serves: 6
Nutrition per serving:
Calories: 491 | Carbs: 45.25 g | Fibres: 8 g | Fat: 31.5 g | Protein: 11.25 g

Ingredients:

- 2 tbsps. extra-virginolive oil
- ½ yellow onion (finely diced)
- 4 garlic cloves (minced)
- 2 cups long-grain rice
- 1 tsp. salt
- 1 tsp. fresh ginger (grated)
- 1 cup water
- 1 cup vegetable stock
- 2 cups coconut milk
- 1 can kidney beans (rinsed and drained)
- 2 tsps. dried thyme
- 1 whole habanero
- Lime (optional)

Preparation:

1. Start by sautéing the onions in a pan over moderate heat. Add the rice and garlic when the onions begin to brown on the edges. Give it 3 minutes to cook while stirring occasionally.

2. Add remaining ingredients and give it a stir to combine. Reduce heat to low and place a lit over the pot. Let cook for 20 minutes or longer until the rice is cooked through. Remove from heat and let sit with the lid on for 10 more minutes.

3. Fluff with a fork and transfer to plates. Drizzle with lime juice! Eat the habanero if you're brave!

Tahini mushroom penne

Prep Time: 5 minutes | Cook time: 15 minutes | Serves: 4
Nutrition per serving:
Calories: 297 | Carbs: 49.25 g | Fibres: 7.75 g | Fat: 7.75 g | Protein: 10.5 g

Ingredients:

- 3 tbsps. maple syrup
- 1 clove garlic (minced)
- 2 tbsps. dark soy sauce
- 1 tbsp. dried spice of choice (rosemary, oregano)

- 500g white button mushrooms (sliced)
- 3 tbsps. tahini
- 160 g whole wheat penne
- 1.6 litre of water
- 1.6 tbsps. of salt

Preparation:

1. Mix the soy sauce, maple syrup, and garlic and dried spice in a bowl.
2. Add the mushrooms to a wok and heat over moderate heat. Add the sauce over the mushrooms. Cover the work with a lid and increase heat to moderate-high. Cook until the mushrooms have released their water.
3. Remove lid and cook the water off while stirring occasionally. Reduce heat and stir in the tahini. Remove from heat!
4. Meanwhile, place the penne in a bowl with 1.6 litres of boiling water and 1.6 tbsps. of salt. Let to cook to instructions. Drain and transfer penne to plates. Pour the mushroom sauce over penne. Decorate with fresh tahini.

Protein-packed tofu stew

Prep Time: 5 minutes | Cook time: 15 minutes | Serves: 4
Nutrition per serving:
Calories: 297 | Carbs: 49.25 g | Fibres: 7.75 g | Fat: 7.75 g | Protein: 10.5 g

Ingredients:

- 2 tbsps. extra-virgin olive oil
- 1 red bell pepper (finely chopped)
- 1 medium yellow onion (finely chopped)
- 1 largesweet potato (peeled and cubed)
- 1 tsp. cumin
- 1 tsp. paprika
- Salt and pepper
- ½ can mixed beans
- 1 cup vegetable broth
- ½ can chopped tomatoes
- 1 bay leaf
- Olive oil spray
- 400 g firm tofu (cubed)
- Fresh coriander

Preparation:

1. Slice the tofu (8 slices) and fry in a pan sprayed with olive oil over moderate heat on both sides. Remove from heat, let cool on a cutting board, and cube to desired size.
2. Heat the olive oil on moderate heat in a wok. Add the bell pepper and onions and let fry for 2-3 minutes. Add the cubed sweet potatoes and seasonings and toss to combine.
3. Stir in the mixed beans, vegetable broth, and chopped tomatoes. Add the bay leaf and let cook for 15 minutes. When nearly done, add in the cubed tofu. Let cook for 5 more minutes. Remove the bay leaf and discard.

4. Serve hot or cold with freshly chopped coriander!

Tip!!! Place the tofu between two plates with a few cans on top to weigh it down and squeeze out the excess water. Pat as dry as possible with kitchen towels.

One-pot curry noodle soup

Prep Time: 10 minutes | Cook time: 20 minutes | Serves: 6
Nutrition per serving:
Calories: 377 | Carbs: 40 g | Fibres: 2 g | Fat: 21 g | Protein: 8 g

Ingredients:

- 2 tbsps.extra-virgin olive oil
- 3 gloves garlic (minced)
- 1 tbsp. ginger (minced)
- 2 tbsps. red curry paste
- 1 can coconut milk (400 ml)
- 3 cups vegetable stock
- 230 g rice noodles
- 200 g firm tofu (well drained and cubed)
- 1 orange bell pepper (sliced or diced finely)
- 2 cups broccoli florets or kale
- Salt to taste
- 1 tbsp. lemon or lime juice
- Finely chopped coriander or parsley to serve

Preparation:

1. Place the olive oil in a large pot over moderate heat. Add the minced ginger and garlic and give it 3 minutes to cook or until fragrant. Add the curry paste, stir, and let cook for 3 more minutes. Reduce heat if necessary so the garlic doesn't burn.
2. Shake the coconut milk can well before opening it. Pour the coconut milk and stir with a spatula until well combined with the curry mixture. Pour the vegetable broth over the coconut milk and curry soup. Bring to a boil.
3. Add the kale or broccoli florets, tofu cubes, and bell pepper slices. Allow 10 minutes to cook. Add the rice noodles and allow 5 more minutes to cook.

4. Season with salt and lime juice to taste. Transfer to bowls and decorate with the chopped parsley or coriander.

Tip!!! You can use any greens for this soup: spinach, broccoli, kale.

Creamy butternut squash risotto

Prep Time: 10 minutes | Cook time: 20 minutes | Serves: 4
Nutrition per serving:
Calories: 327 | Carbs: 61 g | Fibres: 5 g | Fat: 7 g | Protein: 5 g

Ingredients:

- 2 tbsps.extra-virgin olive oil
- 2 cloves garlic (minced)
- 1 tsp. fresh thyme
- 1 yellow onion (finely diced)
- 345 g arborio rice (risotto rice)
- Salt and pepper
- 120 ml dry white wine
- 820 g butternut squash, cubed
- 945 ml vegetable broth
- Fresh parsley or coriander for serving

Preparation:

1. Peel and cube the butternut squash into 2x2 cm pieces. To peel the squash safely, cut the ends off, stab it with a fork, and microwave it for 4 minutes.
2. Heat the oven to 190°C, Mark 6 or 375°F.
3. Place an oven-proof pan on moderate heat with the olive oil. Stir in the onion and let sauté for 3 minutes. When the onions start to become translucent, add the garlic and give it 2 minutes to sauté. Add the thyme and give it 2 more minutes to cook.
4. Add the rice. Sauté for 2 minutes and then add the wine. Season with salt and pepper and add the vegetable stock and butternut squash. Stir to combine and bring to a boil.
5. Remove from heat and place an oven-proof lid over the pot with. Transfer to the pre-heated oven and give it 20 minutes to cook. The rice should have absorbed the liquid. Taste and add more vegetable stock if the rice is not cooked through.

6. Transfer to plates. Decorate with the chopped coriander or parsley and serve immediately!

Tips!!! Substitute butternut squash with sweet potatoes, carrots, swede, or potatoes!

30-Day Vegan Challenge

"A man of my spiritual intensity does not eat corpses"

George Bernard Shaw

The word diet is automatically associated with something that you must do, rather than something that you would like to adopt in order to make your life better. If you want to be successful when completing a diet challenge, you must change your perspective and see the diet as a lifestyle. While a diet comes with restrictions, but a lifestyle comes with benefits. A vegan diet is not a restrictive. You will get all the nutrients you need as long as you avoid animal products. That is really the only restriction.

A vegan challenge is easy to follow, and you will immediately start reaping its benefits. Cooking vegan dishes is so much easier and does not take as much time as omnivorous dishes. Plus, you will get to enjoy the real taste of veggies, unaltered by animal-based products. Going vegan for 30 days will help you sleep better, have more energy, naturally cleanse your body, improve digestion, and reduce your environmental footprint. Most importantly, you will be saving lives. In the long run, the benefits are greater, including lowering the risk of kidney and heart conditions, diabetes type 2, and certain cancers. Start cooking and be vegan!

DAY 1

Breakfast

Coconut milk smoothie

Time: 5 minutes | Serves: 2
Net carbs: 10 g | Fibre: 1 g | Fat: 43 g | Protein: 4 g | Kcal: 415

Ingredients:

- 1 400 g-can coconut milk
- 125 ml frozen blueberries
- 1 tbsp. lemon juice
- ½ tsp. vanilla extract

Preparation:

1. Blend all ingredients to desired consistency. Enjoy!

Lunch

Creamy tomatoes soup

Dinner

Comfort vegan soup

DAY 2

Breakfast

Banana bread American pancakes (Page -)

Lunch

Lentils and roast veggie Lunch salad

Time: 30 minutes | Serves: 2
Carbs: 102 g | Fibre: 18 g | Fat: 8 g | Protein: 28 g | Kcal: 569

Ingredients

- 400 g sweet potatoes (peeled and cubed)
- 200g brussels sprouts (frozen)
- 1 red onion (peeled and cut into wedges)
- Salt and pepper to taste
- 1 tbsp. olive oil
- 1can green lentil (drained and rinsed)
- 700 ml vegetable broth or water
- 1 tbsp. agave syrup
- 3 tbsps. balsamic vinegar
- Freshly chopped parsley for serving

Preparation:

1. Heat the oven to 190°C (380°F).
2. Place the veggies in an oven-proof pan or baking dis. Add the olive oil and sprinkle with salt and pepper. Toss to combine and give it 10 minutes to roast on one side. Flip the veggies and roast for 10 more minutes.
3. Remove veggies from the pan. Transfer veggies to a salad bowl. Add in the rinsed and drained green lentils and toss to combine.
4. Mix the agave syrup, salt and pepper, and balsamic vinegar in a small bowl. Drizzle over the salad and combine to coat the veggies with the dressing. Serve with freshly chopped parsley!

Tips!!! Substitute lentils with chickpeas or kidney beans and the Brussel sprouts with broccoli. Transfer the salad into air-tight containers and refrigerate for up to 5 days.

Dinner

One-pot kidney beans and sweet potatoes stew

DAY 3

Breakfast

Classic avocado toast

Lunch

Oriental lentils salad

Dinner

Vegan mac and cheese

Time: 15 minutes | Serves: 2
Carbs: 101 g | Fibre: 5 g | Fat: 24 g | Protein: 23 g | Kcal: 713

Ingredients:

- 100 g raw cashew nuts
- 1 tbsp. extra-virgin olive oil
- 2 garlic cloves (minced)
- 1 onion (finely chopped)
- 1 roasted red pepper (from jar)
- 1 tbsp. tomato paste
- 2 tbsps. nutritional yeast
- 1 ½ tablespoons corn flour
- 100 g dry pasta (cooked and drained as per directions)
- 500 ml vegetable stock
- Seasonings:
- ½ tsp. smoked paprika
- ½ tsp. turmeric powder
- 1 tsp. ground mustard
- Salt to taste
- For serving:
- Smoked paprika
- Freshly chopped parsley

Preparation:

1. Soak in the cashew nuts in water for at least two hours prior to starting to make this recipe.

2. Heat an oven safe oven on moderate heat. Add the olive oil and stir in the onions and let cook for 3 minutes stirring intermittently. Add minced garlic and let cook for 3 more minutes while stirring.

3. Remove from pot and move into a food processor. Place the tomato paste, red bell pepper, nutritional east, cashews, corn flour, seasonings and vegetable broth into the blender. Pulse to a smooth consistency.

4. Pour the cashew and bell pepper sauce into the pot. Let cook over moderate heat for 5 minutes until it starts thickening. Add the cooked pasta to the saucepan and toss until fully coated.

5. Transfer to plates. Sprinkle with smoked paprika and garnish with fresh parsley. Serve hot! Enjoy!

DAY 4

Breakfast

"Pulled pork" Breakfast sandwich

Time: 30 minutes | Serves: 2
Net carbs: 58 g | Fibre: 2 g | Fat: 4 g | Protein: 1 g | Kcal: 266

Ingredients:

- 1 tbsp. extra-virgin olive oil
- ½ yellow onion (thinly slices)
- 3 cloves garlic (minced)
- 2 cans green jackfruit in water (drained, rinsed, and thinly sliced)
- 1 cup vegetable broth
- ¾ cup vegan barbeque sauce
- Seasonings:
- 1 tsp. ground paprika
- 1 tsp. chili powder
- 1 tsp. ground cumin
- 1 tsp. liquid smoke
- 1 tsp. salt
- 1 tsp. pepper
- For serving:
- red onion slices
- tomato slices
- shredded lettuce
- burger bun

Preparation:

1. Heat the oven to 200ºC (400ºF).
2. Add the garlic and onions in olive oil in a pan over moderate to low heat. Season with salt and pepper and sauté until they become translucent.
3. Add the jackfruit, seasonings, and vegetable stock, and stir to combine. chili powder, paprika, cumin, liquid smoke, salt, pepper, and liquid smoke, and stir. Cook for 15 minutes until the jackfruit is soft.
4. Use two forks to shred the jackfruit. Spread the shredded jackfruit across a baking dish. Place the tray in the oven and give it 25 minutes to cook. Remove from oven and maintain heat.

5. Pour the barbecue sauce over the jackfruit mix. Toss to coat and return to oven. Cook for 10 more minutes.
6. Assemble the burger as per your preference!

Lunch

Roasted veggies bowl

Dinner

Chickpeas curry with rice noodles

DAY 5

Breakfast

Overnight blueberry Breakfast oats

lunch

Pasta and veggie Lunch salad

Time: 15 minutes | Serves: 4

Carbs: 80 g | Fibre: 13 g | Fat: 17 g | Protein: 18 g | Kcal: 542

Ingredients:

- 225 g dried pasta (cooked, drained)
- 150 g tender stem broccoli
- 1 can chickpeas (drained and rinsed)
- 60 g carrot (shredded)
- 75 g red onion (sliced)
- 300 g cherry tomatoes (whole)
- Fresh parsley to taste (chopped)

- Dressing:
- 60 ml olive oil
- 1 clove garlic (minced)
- 60 ml red wine vinegar
- 1 tsp. dried oregano
- Salt and pepper to taste

Preparation:

1. Combine the ingredients for the salad in a bowl.
2. Mix all ingredients for the dressing to combine well.
3. Pour dressing over salad and toss to coat.
4. Enjoy!

Tips!!! This is an easy-to-pack vegan Lunch. Transfer the salad into 4 air-tight containers and refrigerate for up to 5 days. Also, use whole heat pasta for added fiber and protein!Dinner

Curried mushrooms with quinoa

DAY 6

Breakfast

Vegan Breakfast tofu wraps

Lunch

Protein-packed mixed beans salad

Dinner

Quinoa and black beans salad

Time: 30 minutes | Serves: 2
Net carbs: 9 g | Fibre: 8 g | Fat: 47 g | Protein: 15 g | Kcal: 532

Ingredients   :

- 2 tbsps. extra-virgin oliveoil
- 1 jalapeño (finely sliced)
- 3 garlic cloves (minced)
- 425 canned naturally sweetcorn (drained, rinsed)
- 425g canned black beans (drained, rinsed)
- 3 heirloom or Roma tomatoes (finely diced)
- 170 g dry quinoa (rinsed)
- 500 ml vegetable broth
- Seasonings:
- 1 tbsp. ground chili powder
- 2 tsps. ground cumin
- Salt and pepper to taste
- For serving:
- Juice of 1 lime
- Fresh cilantro
- 1 avocado (pitted, cubed)

Preparation:

1. Add the olive oil to a medium-sized frying pan. Heat over moderate heat and fry the garlic and jalapeno. Give it 2 minutes to cook.

2. Add the remaining salad ingredients - black beans, tomatoes, sweetcorn, quinoa, vegetable stock – and seasonings. Stir and give the mixture 20 minutes to cook through with the lid on. The quinoa should be tender and should have already absorbed all the liquid.

3. Transfer the warm salad to bowls. Decorate with the avocado slices, drizzle with lime juice, and top with the avocado, lime juice, and cilantro.

DAY 7

Breakfast

Roasted bell pepper Breakfast soup

Time: 30 minutes | Serves: 1
Carbs: 36 g | Fibre: 6 g | Fat: 11.5 g | Protein: 4 g | Kcal: 150

Ingredients:

- 1 cup of vegetable stock
- 1 garlic clove (minced)
- 3 roasted bell peppers
- Salt and pepper to taste
- Paprika to taste
- Freshly chopped coriander, basil, or parsley

Preparation:

1. Place the roasted bell peppers and garlic in a blender. Pulse into a smooth consistency. Add ½ of vegetable soup. Pulse some more and add more vegetable stock if too thick.
2. Season with salt, pepper, and paprika when you've reached desired consistency. Enjoy with freshly chopped coriander, basil or parsley!

Lunch

Fried tofu with garlicky green beans

Dinner

Stuffed mushrooms with sweet potatoes chips

DAY 8

Breakfast

Low-carb avocado and tofu Breakfast salad

Lunch

Garlicky chickpeas Lunch box

Time: 35 minutes | Serves: 6
Carbs: 42 g | Fibre: 11 g | Fat: 12 g | Protein: 13 g | Kcal: 340

Ingredients:

- 40 g red onion (finely diced)
- 1 can chickpeas (drained and rinsed)
- ½ red bell pepper (diced)
- 3 tablespoons vegan mayonnaise
- Seasonings:
- ½ tsp. Dijon mustard
- ½ tsp. garlic powder
- ½ tsp. onion powder
- 1 tbsp. fresh dill
- Salt and pepper to taste
- For serving:
- Leafy greens
- Sliced bread

Preparation:

1. Mash the chickpeas to a coarse consistency with a potato masher in a medium bowl. Add the chopped red onion, vegan mayo, diced red pepper, and seasonings. Stir until well-combined.
2. Spread on vegan bread of choice and top with greens of choice! Enjoy!

Dinner

Jamaican rice and beans

DAY 9

Breakfast

Spinach whole-wheat tortilla wraps

Lunch

Greens and potatoes skillet

Dinner

Low-carb broccoli soup

Time: 20 minutes | Serves: 4

Net carbs: 10 g | Fibre: 2.8 g | Fat: 54 g | Protein: 7.2 g | Kcal: 551

Ingredients:

- 1 leek (finely sliced)
- 300 g broccoli (florets)
- 1 vegetable bouillon cube
- ½ litre water
- salt
- 400 ml coconut milk cream
- fresh basil
- 1 garlic clove (minced)
- Black pepper

Preparation:

1. Bring a pot with the water to a gentle boil. Add the leeks, broccoli, vegetable stock and cook with a lid on for 2 minutes so that broccoli is tender. Remove from heat!
2. Blend the soup with an immersion blender. Add the coconut milk, garlic, and black pepper. Blend to combine.
3. Transfer the soup to bowls. Serve with freshly chopped basil!

DAY 10

Breakfast

Gingery spinach coconut smoothie

Time: 5 minutes | Serves: 2
Net carbs: 3 g | Fibre: 1 g | Fat: 8 g | Protein: 1 g | Kcal: 82

Ingredients:

- 150 ml water
- 2 tsp. fresh ginger (grated)
- 75 ml coconut cream
- 30 g frozen spinach
- 2 tbsp. lemon juice

Preparation:

1. Add the ingredients for the smoothie to a blender and process to desired consistency. Adjust to taste with lemon juice.

Lunch

Vegan swede and pumpkin soup

Dinner

Tahini mushrooms penne

DAY 11

Breakfast

Overnight raspberry pudding

Lunch

Creamy courgette salad

Time: 15 minutes | Serves: 1
Net carbs: 8 g | Fibre: 7 g | Fat: 54 g | Protein: 8 g | Kcal: 556

Ingredients:

- 1 tbsp. olive oil
- 2 courgettes
- salt and pepper
- 1 Romaine lettuce head
- 110g rocket leaves
- ¾ cup roasted pecans (chopped)
- Vegan mayo dressing

- 180 ml vegan mayonnaise
- 2 tbsp olive oil
- 1 garlic clove
- 2 tsp. lemon juice
- ¼ tsp chili powder
- ½ tsp. salt

Preparation:

1. Slice the courgette in halves lengthwise. Spoon out the seeds and cut crosswise to bite-size pieces. Slice the romaine lettuce to desired size.
2. Add the courgette to a frying pan with shimmering olive oil. Season with salt and pepper and cook until golden. Remove from heat.

3. Add the lettuce and rocket to a salad bowl. Mix in the sautéed courgette and chopped roasted pecan nuts.

4. Whisk together the ingredients for the vegan mayo dressing. Add the dressing to the salad bowl and toss to combine. Enjoy!

Dinner

Protein-packed tofu stew

DAY 12

Breakfast

Vegan chickpea omelette

lunch

Quinoa tabbouleh

Dinner

Vegan fettucine pasta

Time: 20 minutes | Serves: 2
Carbs: 55 g | Fibre: 5 g | Fat: 21 g | Protein: 17 g | Kcal: 470

Ingredients:

- 1 cup raw cashews
- 3 cups boiling water
- ¾ cup water at room temperature
- ½ medium onion (finely diced)
- 3 cloves garlic
- 3 tbsps.nutritional yeast
- 1 tsp. pepper
- 1 tsp. dried rosemary
- 1 tsp. salt
- 1 tsp. lemon juice
- 1 box vegan pasta (cooked)
- fresh parsley (chopped)

Preparation:

1. Place the cashew nuts in a small pot and add the boiling water. Place a lid over the bowl and give the nuts 15 minutes to soak. Drain and transfer to a blender.
2. Add the room temperature water, nutritional yeast, garlic, onions, and seasonings to the blender. Pulse to smooth consistency.
3. Place the cooked pasta onto plates. Add the cashew sauce and mix with the pasta to coat. Decorate with freshly chopped parsley.

DAY 13

Vegan chocolate mousse

Time: 20 minutes | Serves: 3
Carbs: 54 g | Fibre: 11 g | Fat: 14 g | Protein: 13 g | Kcal: 377

Ingredients:

- Aquafaba of 1 can of chickpeas
- ½ cup vegan chocolate (melted)
- 2 tbsps. sugar
- 1 tsp. vanilla extract

Preparation:

1. In a medium-sized bowl, whisk the water yielded by 1 can of chickpeas until soft peaks form.
2. Add in the melted vegan chocolate, vanilla extract, and sugar. Fold in gently but do not overmix. Transfer to serving cups and refrigerate overnight.
3. The next morning, decorate with fresh raspberries and enjoy!

Lunch

Balkan aubergines salad

Dinner

One-pot curry noodle soup

DAY 14

Breakfast

Vegan raspberry ice cream

Lunch

Avocado and roasted chickpeas salad

Time: 30 minutes | Serves: 4
Carbs: 41 g | Fibre: 12 g | Fat: 12 g | Protein: 13 g | Kcal: 326

Ingredients:

- 150g mixed greens
- 1 large cucumber (seeded, diced)
- 275g cherry tomato halves
- 1 avocado (pitted, diced)
- Roasted chickpeas:
- 2 tbsps. olive oil
- 2 cans chickpeas (drained and rinsed)

- 2 tsps. smoked paprika
- 1 ½ tsps. garlic salt
- Dressing:
- 2 tbsps. extra-virgin olive oil
- 2 tbsps. lemon juice
- Freshly chopped parsley
- ½ tsp. salt

Preparation:

1. Preheat the oven to 200°C (400°F). Mix the chickpeas with the seasonings and olive oil in a large bowl. Spread uniformly onto a baking tray and let roast for 20-30 until crispy. Remove from oven. Transfer to a salad bowl.
2. Toss in diced cucumber, mixed greens, tomato halves, and avocado cubes. Mix the dressing ingredients and add over the salad. Toss to combine. Adjust seasoning to taste.

3. Serve salad in bowls and enjoy with freshly chopped parsley!

Dinner

Creamy butternut squash risotto

DAY 15

Breakfast

Breakfast quinoa bowl

Lunch

Refreshing brown rice salad

Dinner

Vegan fried cauliflower rice

Time: 20 minutes | Serves: 2
Net carbs: 15 g | Fibre: 6 g | Fat: 62 g | Protein: 18.5 g | Kcal: 698

Ingredients:

- 450 g cauliflower rice
- 110 g olive oil
- ½ green bell pepper (finely sliced)
- ½ yellow onion (finely sliced)
- 50 g green onions (finely sliced)
- 1 red chili pepper (finely sliced)
- 2 garlic cloves (minced)
- 30 g fresh ginger (grated)
- 1 tbsp. sesame oil
- 200 g soft tofu (crumbled)
- salt and pepper

Preparation:

1. Place the olive oil in a pan over moderate to high heat. Add onions, green onion, bell pepper, cauliflower, and chilli. Stir fry until the cauliflower is slightly golden.
2. Stir the ginger along with the garlic in the cauliflower mixture. Stir to combine. Lower the heat and add in the sesame oil. Season to taste. Stir to combine.
3. Add the tofu over the cauliflower mixture. Stir to combine and give it 1-3 minutes to cook through.
4. Transfer to plates and serve hot!

DAY 16

Breakfast

Nutty spinach on avocado toast

Time: 15 minutes | Serves: 2
Carbs: 27.5 g | Fibre: 9.5 | Fat: 28.5 g | Protein: 8 g | Kcal: 379

Ingredients:

- 2 tbsps. olive oil
- 1 garlic glove (minced)
- 1 small red onion (julienned)
- 200 g baby spinach (chopped)
- 1 tbsp. tomato paste
- Finely chopped fresh dill
- 2 small avocados circa 80 g each (pitted, halved)
- 3 walnut halves
- 4 slices multigrain crispbread thins
- Salt and pepper

Preparation:

1. Heat the olive oil in a wok on moderate heat. Add the red onion and garlic. Stir and let fry until the garlic is fragrant and onion is translucent.
2. Add the spinach to the wok with the onion and garlic. When the spinach has slightly wilted, stir in the tomato paste and season to taste. Increase heat and give the spinach mixture 5 minutes to simmer or until all the liquid has evaporated.
3. Place the avocados in a bowl and mash with a fork to desired consistency. Season with salt and pepper. Spread the avocado on top of the crispbread. Top with the spinach mixture and sprinkle with crushed walnuts.
4. Enjoy immediately!

Lunch

Creamy tomatoes soup

Dinner

Comfort vegan stew

DAY 17

Breakfast

Banana bread American pancakes

Lunch

Warm and creamy broccoli soup

Time: 30 minutes | Serves: 2

Carbs: 83 g | Fibre: 0.75 g | Fat: 1.85 g | Protein: 17.5 g | Kcal: 394

Ingredients:

- 2 large potatoes (peeled and sliced)
- 1 large broccoli head (cut into small pieces)
- Vegetable broth as needed
- 100g baby spinach
- Freshly chopped parsley
- Salt and pepper to taste

Preparation:

1. Add the broccoli to a pot of lightly salted boiling water and let cook until the broccoli is fork tender. Remove from water and transfer to a food processor.
2. Meanwhile, add the potatoes into a pot of boiling water. Let cook until fork tender. Remove from water and transfer to the same food processor.
3. Add 1 cup of vegetable broth and pulse to a smooth consistency. Add more vegetable broth depending on desired thickness. Season with salt and pepper to taste.
4. Transfer the soup to a pot over moderate heat. Add in the baby spinach leaves and let simmer until the spinach has wilted. Stir to combine. Taste and season if needed.
5. Enjoy hot with freshly chopped parsley! Add a dollop of coconut milk for extra flavour!

Dinner

Chickpea curry with rice noodles

DAY 18

Breakfast

Classic avocado toast

Lunch

Oriental lentils salad

Dinner

Courgettes pasta mushroom stroganoff

Time: 30 minutes | Serves: 2

Carbs: 56 g | Fibre: 7 g | Fat: 27.5 g | Protein: 8 g | Kcal: 476

Ingredients:

- 1 tbsp. extra-virgin olive oil
- 500 g chestnut mushrooms (quartered)
- 1 tbsp. dried thyme
- 350 ml coconut cream
- Cayenne pepper to taste (optional)
- Salt and pepper to taste

- Courgettes pasta:
- 2 courgettes
- 1 tbsp. extra-virgin olive oil
- Salt and pepper to taste
- Lemon juice to taste (optional)
- Freshly chopped dill for serving

Preparation:

1. Sauté the mushrooms in the olive oil in a saucepan over moderate to high heat. Stir occasionally until the water yielded by the mushrooms has cooked off.
2. Add the coconut cream to the same saucepan and reduce heat. Let the mushroom and coconut cream sauce cook to desired thickness. Salt and pepper to taste! For a hot stroganoff, stir in cayenne pepper.

3. While the stroganoff is cooking, cut the courgette lengthwise in fettucine-like slices and add to a pot of boiling water that has been previously salted. Give it 1 minute to boil. Drain well and transfer to plates.

4. Drizzle olive oil over the courgette fettucine and season to taste. Top the courgette paste with the stroganoff mushrooms. Decorate with freshly chopped dill and serve hot! Enjoy!

DAY 19

Breakfast

Classic humous and veggies sandwich

Time: 5 minutes | Serves: 2
Carbs: 46.5 g | Fibre: 14 g | Fat: 19 g | Protein: 14 g | Kcal: 411

Ingredients:

- Humous:
- 1 can chickpeas (drained and rinsed)
- ½ tsp. salt
- ½ tsp. ground cumin
- 1 clove garlic, minced
- 1 tbsp. extra virgin olive oil
- 1 tbsp. lemon juice

- 2 tbsps. tahini
- 60 ml or more of water
- More lemon juice to taste
- For the sandwich:
- 8 Finn Crisp classic thins
- Tomato slices
- Cucumber slices

Preparation:

1. Place the chickpeas on one half of a kitchen towel and fold the over the other half. Rub the beans until most of the skins have come off.
2. Add all the humous ingredients, except for the tahini, to a food processor. Start blending and add the tahini while the processor is running. Blend to a smooth consistency. Taste and adjust seasoning to preference.
3. Spread the humous on the crispbread thins and top with tomato and cucumber slices! Enjoy!

Lunch

Roasted veggies bowl

Dinner

Curried mushrooms with quinoa

DAY 20

Breakfast

Overnight blueberry Breakfast oats

Lunch

Vegan spaghetti carbonara

Time: 30 minutes | Serves: 4
Carbs: 73 g | Fibre: 5 g | Fat: 17 g | Protein: 15 g | Kcal: 503

Ingredients:

- 340 g spaghetti (wholegrain)
- 225g shiitake mushrooms
- 3 tbsps. olive oil
- Seasonings:
- ½ tsp. smoked paprika
- ½ tsp. salt
- ¼ tsp. pepper
- Carbonara sauce:
- 60 ml olive oil
- 65 g cashews, soaked overnight
- 80 ml plant-based milk (unsweetened)
- 3 garlic cloves (minced)
- 1 ½ tbsps. lemon juice
- 1 ½ tbsps. nutritional yeast
- ¼ tsp. paprika
- Salt and pepper to taste
- fresh parsley, for serving

Preparation:

1. Heat oven to 190°C (375°F).
2. **Shiitake bacon:** Slice the shiitake mushrooms finely and place in a bowl with the olive oil and seasonings. Toss to coat evenly and transfer to a baking trained lined with baking sheet. Transfer to oven and give it 14-16 minutes to bake flipping halfway. Mushrooms should be brown and crispy. Let the mushroom „bacon" cool on the baking tray.

3. ***Carbonara sauce:*** Add all carbonara sauce ingredients to a food processor and blend into a creamy and smooth paste. Taste and adjust seasoning to preference.

4. Meanwhile, cook pasta as per directions. Drain and return to pot. Pour the chickpeas sauce over the spaghetti and stir to coat the pasta evenly. Transfer to plates and serve topped with the mushroom

5. Mix in mushroom bacon. op with parsley.

Dinner

Stuffed mushrooms with sweet potato chips

DAY 21

Breakfast

Vegan Breakfast tofu wraps

Lunch

Protein-packed mixed beans salad

Dinner

Vegan lasagne soup

Time: 30 minutes | Serves: 6
Net carbs: 32 g | Fibre: 4 g | Fat: 3 g | Protein: 9 g | Kcal: 235

Ingredients:

- 1 tbsp. extra-virgin olive oil
- 3 cloves garlic (minced)
- 2 tbsps. tomato paste
- 1 yellow onion (diced)
- 1 tsp. dried oregano
- 1 tsp. dried basil
- 2 cans chopped tomatoes
- 50 g dry green lentil (rinsed)
- 1.5 l vegetable broth
- 225 g lasagne noodle (uncooked, broken into 5 cm pieces)
- 150 g spinach
- fresh basil for serving

Preparation:

1. Heat the olive oil in a large pot on moderate heat an fry the onion for 3 minutes. Add the garlic, seasonings, and tomato paste to the pan. Give it 3 more minutes to cook and become fragrant.

2. Stir in the lentils, chopped tomatoes, and vegetable broth and give it time to come to a gentle boil. Once boiling, increase heat to high and give it 10 more minutes to cook. The lentils should not be fully cooked.

3. Add in the lasagne noodles pieces and let cook whole stirring occasionally until the lentils is tender and the lasagne noodles are cooked through. It should take about 15 minutes.
4. Finally, add the spinach to the hot pot and give it a couple of minutes to wilt. Transfer to bowls and serve hot topped with freshly chopped basil!

DAY 22

Humous potato boats

Time: 50 minutes | Servings: 10
Carbs: 29 g | Fibre: 5 g | Fat: 2 g | Protein: 5 g | Kcal: 157

Ingredients:

- Potatoes:
- 10 small yellow potatoes (skin on, halved)
- Olive oil spray
- Salt and pepper to taste
- Filling:
- 1 can chickpeas
- 2 tsp. Dijon mustard
- 1 tbsp. lemon juice
- 1 tsp. turmeric powder

- 1 tbsp. garlic powder
- 1 tsp. ground cumin
- 1 tsp. cayenne pepper (optional)
- 2 tbsps. or more water
- 2 tbsps. tahini sauce
- Salt and pepper to taste
- Serving:
- Paprika to taste
- freshly chopped parsley (chives) to taste

Preparation:

1. Potatoes: Heat oven to 190°C (380°F). Place the potato halves skin down on an oven-safe tray previously lined with baking paper. Season with salt and pepper and spray with olive oil. Bake the potatoes halves for 40 minutes, or until soft.

2. Remove tray from oven and spoon out a small portion of the central section of each potato half. The goal is to create a small bowl. Place the scooped-out potato flesh into a food processor.

3. **Humous centre:** Add the rest of the ingredients for the filling to the blender along with the potato flash. Turn on the processor and blend into a creamy, smooth humous. Use a piping bag to fill the potato cups with the humous mix.

4. Arrange potato halves on plates and serve with smoked paprika and freshly chopped parsley (or chives).

lunch

Fried tofu with garlicky green beans

Dinner

Jamaican rice and beans

DAY 23

Breakfast

Low-carb avocado and tofu Breakfast salad

Lunch

Budget-friendly vegan "noodles"

Time: 30 minutes | Serves: 4
Carbs: 60 g | Fibre: 5 g | Fat: 26 g | Protein: 19 g | Kcal: 540

Ingredients:

- Dressing:
- 120 g peanut butter
- 2 tbsps. sesame oil
- 3 tbsps. dark soy sauce
- 2 tbsps. rice vinegar
- 3 tbsps. water
- 2 ½ tsps. brown sugar
- 1 clove garlic
- ½ tbsp. fresh ginger, minced

- Spaghetti and veggies:
- 240 g spaghetti
- 55 g carrot (grated)
- 115 g edamame (shelled)
- 50 g red cabbage (very finely sliced)
- For serving:
- Peanuts or nuts of choice
- Black sesame seeds

Finely sliced scallions

Preparation:

1. Cook pasta according to package instructions. Drain the vegan pasta and transfer to a large bowl. Add the edamame, carrots, and cabbage over the pasta. Set aside.
2. Mix all dressing ingredients in a food processor until they form a smooth, creamy sauce. Taste and adjust seasoning to preference!

3. Pour the peanut butter sauce over the spaghetti and veggies. Mix with tongs until the pasta and vegs are well coated. Divide into serving bowls and top with sliced scallions, peanuts, and black sesame seeds!

Tip!!! Use wholegrain pasta of choice! Substitute scallions with chopped parsley, basil, or coriander. Substitute peanuts with nuts of choice!

Dinner

Protein-packed tofu stew

DAY 24

Breakfast

Spinach whole-wheat tortilla wraps

Lunch

Greens and potatoes skillet

Dinner

Vegan cheat burgers

Time: 25 minutes | Serves: 5

Carbs: 43 g | Fibre: 8 g | Fat: 2 g | Protein: 16 g | Kcal per patty: 228

!!!Bun and fixings not included in calorie calculation!!!

Ingredients:

- 1 can chickpeas (unsalted, drained and rinsed)
- 1 medium sweet potato (cooked and peeled)
- 1 clove garlic (minced)
- 1 tsp. chili powder
- ½ tsp. salt
- 25 g scallions (chopped)
- 35 g cornmeal
- 70g BBQ sauce (see recipe below)
- Barbeque sauce:
- 60 ml water
- 2 tbsps. apple cider vinegar

- 170 g tomato paste
- 2 tbsps. maple syrup
- ½ tsp. garlic powder
- ¼ tsp. salt
- ½ tsp. chili powder
- Optional Fixings:

Preparation:

1. Heat oven to 190°C (375°F).
2. ***Burger patties:*** Place the chickpeas and seasonings in a large mixing bowl. Add the seasonings and sweet potato and mash with a potato masher to a fine texture. Add the scallions and the cornmeal and mix until well combined. Set aside.
3. ***Barbecue sauce:*** Mix all barbecue sauce ingredients in a medium bowl. Adjust seasonings to preference.
4. ***Burger patties:*** Pour 70 g of the BBQ sauce over the burger patties mixture and mix to combine well. Create 5 patties from the mixture and arrange on a sheet pan lined with parchment paper. Place the sheet pan in the oven and roast for 40 minutes, flipping over halfway.
5. ***Burgers:*** Serve the vegan burgers with the BBQ sauce, favourite addons, and hot buns.

DAY 25

Breakfast

Tofu nuggets

Time: 10 minutes | Serves: 1
Net carbs: 18 g | Fibre: 2 g | Fat: 22 g | Protein: 10 g | Kcal: 331

Ingredients:

- 180g vegan mayonnaise
- 400 g tofu (drained and cubed)
- 85 g breadcrumbs
- 2 tbsps. nutritional yeast
- 1 tsp. garlic powder
- Salt and pepper to taste
- 1 tsp. paprika

Preparation:

1. Heat the oven to 200ºC (400ºF). Place a wire rack over a baking tray lined with baking sheet and set aside.
2. Place the vegan mayo in a bowl. In a separate bowl, add the rest of the ingredients, except for the tofu, and mix until combined.
3. Coat each tofu cube with mayonnaise and then put through the bread crumb mixture to coat evenly. Add the breadcrumb-covered tofu cubes to the wire rack. Transfer to oven and let bake for 30-40 minutes. Remove from oven and give it 5 minutes to cool.
4. Serve with humous, vegan barbecue sauce,

Lunch

Vegan swede and pumpkin soup

Dinner

Tahini mushroom penne

DAY 26

Breakfast

Overnight raspberry pudding

Lunch

Creamy shiitake mushrooms on cous-cous bed

Time: 15 minutes | Serves: 3
Carbs: 67 g | Fibre: 5.6 g | Fat: 11 g | Protein: 9.6 g | Kcal: 394

Ingredients:

- 1 tbsp. olive oil
- 300 g shiitake mushrooms (finely sliced)
- ½ tsp. garlic powder
- ½ tsp. cayenne pepper
- ½ tsp. garam masala
- ½ tsp. white pepper
- Salt to taste
- 100 g coconut cream
- 1 cup dry couscous
- Fresh parsley to garnish

Preparation:

1. Heat olive oil in a medium wok over moderate heat. Add the shiitake mushrooms to the work with the shimmering oil. Stir and give it 2-3 minutes to fry. Stir in the seasonings and give it 1 more minute to cook.
2. Add in the solid part of the coconut cream. Stir and allow 5 more minutes to cook. Taste and adjust seasoning accordingly. Remove from heat.
3. Meanwhile, cook the couscous as per package instructions. Arrange on two plates. Top with the creamy shiitake mushrooms and garnish with freshly chopped parsley!

Dinner

One-pot curry noddle soup

DAY 27

Breakfast

Vegan chickpea omelette

Lunch

Quinoa tabbouleh

Dinner

Vegan shepherd's pie

Time: 20 minutes | Serves: 2
Carbs: 19 g | Fibre: 2 g | Fat: 13 g | Protein: 2 g | Kcal: 108

Ingredients:

- 4 russet potatoes (peeled and boiled)
- Plant-based milk as needed
- Vegan butter as needed
- Salt and pepper
- Veggie filling:
- 1 tbsp. olive oil
- 3 carrots (finely diced)
- 3 stalks celery (finely chopped)
- ½ yellow onion (finely diced)
- 150 g chopped mushrooms (150 g)
- 1 tbsp. flour
- 1 tsp. thyme (fresh)
- 1 tsp. sage (fresh)
- 4 cloves garlic
- 475 vegetable broth
- 80 ml red wine
- 1 tbsp. tomato paste
- Cooking oil spray

Preparation:

1. Veggie filling: Heat the olive oil over moderate heat in a medium saucepan. Add the onion, carrots, and celery to the pan. Sauté for a couple of minutes.

2. Add the mushrooms and fry for two more minutes. Stir in the flour, tomato paste, garlic, sage, thyme, and season with salt and pepper.

3. Stir in the wine and vegetable broth. Gently stir to incorporate and let simmer for 10 minutes to thicken.

4. *Mash:* Use a potato masher to mash the potatoes. Mix in the vegan butter, and plant-based milk. Mix to a smooth consistency and season with salt and pepper to preference.

5. *Shepherd Pie:* in a baking sheet, place the veggie filling in an even layer. Add the mash on top and create a pattern of choice on the top to make the surface crispier when cooked. When done, spray cooking spray over.

6. Place the pie under the broiler. Let it cook for 15 minutes or until the surface has become crispy. Enjoy!

DAY 28

Breakfast

Two-ways Breakfast muffins

Time: 30 minutes | Serves: 12

Net carbs: 30 g | Fibre: 6.6 g | Fat: 17.5 g | Protein: 8.33 g | Kcal: 232

Ingredients:

- 9 ripe bananas
- 150 g blueberry
- 60 g cocoa powder
- 360 g nut butter of choice

Preparation:

1. Heat the oven to 180°C (350°F).
2. Use a fork to mash the bananas. Mix in the nut butter until well combined. Place ½ of the batter into one bowl and the remaining half into a separate bowl.
3. *Cocoa muffins:* Incorporate the cocoa powder into the first bowl.
4. *Blueberry muffins:* Incorporate the blueberries into the second bowl.
5. Pour the cocoa batter into 6 cups of the muffin tin. Pour the blueberry batter into 6 cups of the muffin tin. Transfer to muffins and bake for 20 minutes. Let muffins cool.

Lunch

Balkan aubergine salad

Dinner

Creamy butternut squash risotto

DAY 29

Breakfast

Vegan raspberry ice cream

Lunch

Rich buddha bowl with tahini dressing

Time: 15 minutes | Serves: 4
Net carbs: 3.5 g | Fibre: 7 g | Fat: 48 g | Protein: 17 g | Kcal: 525

Ingredients:

- Dressing for baking:
- 2 ½ tbsps. olive oil
- ½ tsp. onion powder
- 2 garlic cloves, minced
- ½ tsp. cumin
- ½ tsp. paprika
- Roasted veggies:
- 200 g butternut squash (peeled, diced)
- 75 g mushroom (diced)
- 100 g Brussel sprout (halved)
- Salt and pepper to taste
- Buddha bowl:
- 135 g kale
- 50g red cabbage (diced)
- 510 g quinoa (cooked)
- 100 g beet (cooked, diced)
- 200 g canned lentils (drained)
- 50g walnuts
- Tahini dressing:
- 1 tbsp. maple syrup
- 75 g tahini
- 1 tbsp. apple cider
- 2 tbsps. water
- 1 tbsp. fresh orange juice
- Pinch of salt and pepper
- For serving:
- Fresh herb of choice

Preparation:

1. Preheat the oven to 200°C (400°F).
2. **Dressing for roasting:** Mix all ingredients for the dressing for baking into a bowl. Set aside.
3. **Roasted veggies:** Add the mushrooms, butternut squash, and Brussel sprouts to an oven-proof tray. Season with the dressing. Salt and pepper to taste. Mix the veggies on the tray until well coated. Transfer to oven. Give the veggies 25 minutes to roast.
4. **Tahini dressing:** Combine all ingredients for the salad dressing in a bowl. Set aside.
5. Arrange the remaining buddha bowl ingredients along with the roasted veggies in a large bowl. Drizzle the tahini dressing over the salad. Serve with freshly chopped herb of choice!

Dinner

One-pot kidney beans and sweet potatoes stew

DAY 30

Breakfast

Breakfast quinoa bowl

Lunch

Refreshing brown rice salad

Dinner

Creamy "cheddar" broccoli soup

Time: 30 minutes | Serves: 4
Net carbs: 12 g | Fibre: 9 g | Fat: 65 g | Protein: 38 g | Kcal: 821

Ingredients:

- 1 tbsp. olive oil
- 1 medium yellow onion (finely chopped)
- 3 carrots (sliced)
- 2 potatoes (cubed)
- 3 garlic cloves (minced)
- 500 ml vegetable broth
- salt, to taste
- 1 head broccoli florets (roasted or steamed)
- "Cheddar" sauce:
- 65 g cashew nuts socked overnight
- 900 ml vegetable broth
- 70 g nutritional yeast
- 1 tsp. paprika
- 1 tsp. pepper
- Freshly chopped parsley

Preparation:

1. Place the oil in a large pot over moderate heat. Add the onion and give it 5 minutes to become translucent. Add the potatoes, carrots, and garlic. Season with salt and add 500 ml of vegetable broth. Place a lid over the pot and give the veggie soup 30 minutes to simmer.

2. Move the soup to a food processor and blend to a smooth consistency. Return to pot.
3. Rinse the blender. Add the cashew nuts, remaining soup, nutritional yeas pepper and paprika to the blender. Blend to a smooth consistency. Taste and adjust seasonings to preference.
4. Add the cashew cheese sauce to the pot with the soup. Add the broccoli florets to the soup. Give it a quick stir. Serve hot and garnish with freshly chopped parsley!

Disclaimer

The opinions and ideas of the author contained in this publication are designed to educate the reader in an informative and helpful manner. While we accept that the instructions will not suit every reader, it is only to be expected that the recipes might not gel with everyone. Use the book responsibly and at your own risk. This work with all its contents, does not guarantee correctness, completion, quality or correctness of the provided information. Always check with your medical practitioner should you be unsure whether to follow a low carb eating plan. Misinformation or misprints cannot be completely eliminated. Human error is real!

Imprint

Printed in Great Britain
by Amazon